*THE ALL NEW STYLE OF MAGAZINE-BOOKS*

**SDM**

www.SDMLIVE.com

**MP**

MOCY PUBLISHING
WWW.MOCYPUBLISHING.COM

CDXTREME
Worldwide Distribution. Get Paid Monthly.
SIGN-UP FOR FREE TODAY!!!
Why Sign Your Music with a Record Label.
Get Your Music on iTunes, Amazon, Tidal and other Major online Stores Worldwide!
$7.99 PER SINGLE
$29.99 PER EP ALBUM
$39.99 PER LP ALBUM
FREE UPC BARCODES and ISRC CODES
Get online and register your music at:
WWW.CDXTREME.COM

REAL MUSIC. REAL ENTERTAINMENT.

# SDM

ISSUE 3

**ALSO**
**AUHMAZ!N**
**ISHMAELSOUL**
**MZ. PLATINUM**
**KID JAY**

## KOSTA
### JUST HIT THE JACKPOT WITH A NEW SMASH HIT SINGLE "LOTTERY"

## BIGG DAWG BLAST
### LAUNCHES THE STREET HITTA DJ'S MOVEMENT

# Neisha Neshae

### BRINGING IN 2016 ON STAGE WITH THE KING OF R&B R-KELLY & DROPPING A NEW MIXTAPE

## THE RED CARPET EDITION
### SUPERSTARS CAME WITH FASHION AT THE SDM MAGAZINE RELEASE PARTY

**PLUS MORE**

US - $9.99  CANADA - $14.99

01 >

9 770317 847001

JANUARY 2016 No.3
WWW.SDMLIVE.COM

# SDM

**EDITOR-IN-CHIEF**
D. "Casino" Bailey
casino@sdmlive.com

**EDITORAL DIRECTOR**
Sheree Cranford
sheree@sdmlive.com

**GRAPHIC/WEB DESIGNER**
D. "Casino" Bailey
casino@sdmlive.com

**A&R MANAGER**
Aye Money
ayemoney@sdmlive.com

**ACCOUNT EXECUTIVE**
Frank Harvest Jr.
frank@sdmlive.com

**PHOTOGRAPHERS**
Treagen Colston
D. "Casino" Bailey

**CONTRIBUTORS**
April Smiley
Courtney Benjamin

**COPY ORDERS & ADVERTISING OFFICE**
**Send Money Order or Check to:**
Mocy Publishing
P.O. Box 35195
Detroit, Michigan 48235
(586) 646-8505
advertise@sdmlive.com

**Copy Order Item #:**
SDM Magazine Issue #6 2016
S&H Plus Retail Price - $9.99 per copy

**WWW.SDMLIVE.COM**

**Printed by CreateSpace, An Amazon.com Company**

SDM

REAL MUSIC. REAL ENTERTAINMENT.

ISSUE 6

ALSO
GUCCI RIE
WOODROW
HICKSGATE
TERRY MARTIN
RJ SCOTT
+MORE

**FRESH MONEY DA MAC**
RAPPER GOES SOLO AFTER MUSIC DEAL WITH SOULJA BOY

**MOBDIVA**
LIFE AFTER TELEVISION NOW LIVING RICH AND FAMOUS HIT SINGLE

**JP ONE**
SOUTHWEST DETROIT KING GIVES SDM THE SCOOP ON FAKE INDUSTRY RAPPERS AND THE BIRTH OF HIS NEW DIRECTION

# CONTENTS

**1**

**SiriusXM - SD2 Portable Speaker Dock**
$109.99
www.bestbuy.com

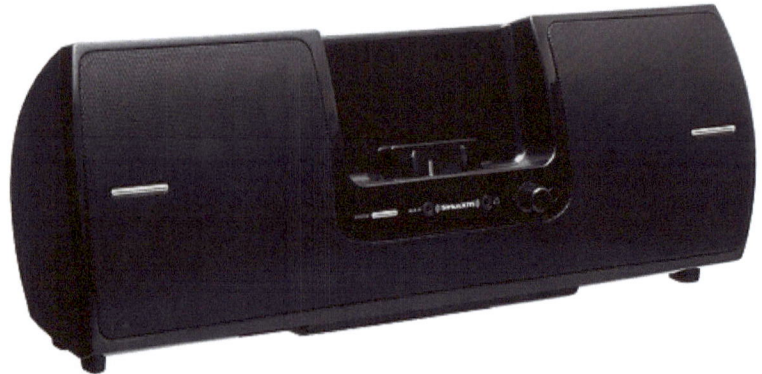

**2**

**Power Acoustik - Hdvd-71Cc Universal Headrest Monitor With DVD ,7"**
$144.99
www.bestbuy.com

**3**

**Apple - Apple Watch 42mm Stainless Steel case - Medium Storm Gray Leather Loop Band**
$699.99
www.apple.com

# Bad Boy Welcomes a New Member

IT'S A NEW ERA OF HIP HOP AS P. DIDDY SIGNS HIS SON CHRISTIAN COMBS TO BAD BOY RECORDS AS A NEW ARTIST.

by Cheraee C.

The Bad Boy camp just keeps on getting larger and larger. This past weekend P. Diddy gifted his son Christian Combs with a contract to the label for his eighteenth birthday. Back in October, Bad Boy joined Epic Records so the CEO LA Reid was present also to share this wonderful experience.

P. Diddy has posted all about his son joining forces with Bad Boy on every social media outlet there is including Snapchat so it's clear this is definitely a proud father moment, as well as a memorable business moment especially since he is quite the mega mogul in many trades. One thing's for sure, he believes in young talent and the next generation of hip hop. He wants to find the next Biggie, the next P. Diddy, the next Tupac, or the next Lil Kim, not just an artist who can makes ` music, but an artist who can change the industry and then takeover other industries as well. With P. Diddy taking the wheel, it won't be long before Christian will be like father like son, but since this is the next generation, Christian has the potential to be even greater then his father. Let's keep welcoming Christian to Bad Boy Records.

Christian Combs

Happiness is a choice

#JustSoYouKnow

# A Stage Play and Book Release

RASHELLE REY RELEASES HER NEW BOOK "I AM WHAT GOD SAYS I AM..." AND STAGE PLAY IN THE SAME DAY.

by Cheraee C.

In today's society there are all types of devilish issues that people encounter, experience, and suppress. Rashelle Rey reflects on some of those major issues in her new book and gives personal experiences, scriptures from the Bible, and more to motivate inner peace. She describes issues like sexual abuse, drugs, and spirituality, and the things we use to suppress these issues such as gambling, food, clothes, makeup, money, and more. It's time that people stop running from their issues and face them. Rashelle's new book is the perfect way to get encouraged, and if reading isn't your style, then you should definitely go check out her stage play.

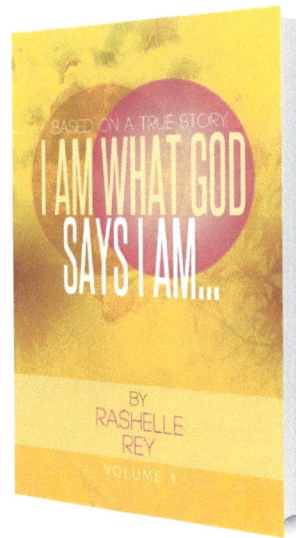

**I Am What God Says I Am...**
*By Rashelle Rey*

*Available from Amazon.com and other online stores*

# Who is Fresh Money Da Mac?

**FRESH MONEY** GOT THE STREETS AND HE'S FEELING LIKE A CHAMPION WITH HIS NEW HIT SINGLE "CHAMPION".

**by Cheraee C.**

**Q. How long have you been in the music world and who put you on?**

A. I've been making music for 7 years. I started off my music career in a group called The Hurricane Boyz. We won a contest on Souljaboy's website which got us a lot of attention. After constantly dropping music, it felt as if our music wasn't reaching enough people so we reached out to my current manager Rick Lawrence (RL Entertainment) for management. We emailed Rick our song and he immediately called us and said that we had potential and wanted to take us under his wing in camp. His boot camp consisted of us rehearsing, recording, working out, and numerous other things everyday. With less then a month of artist boot camp and little experience on stage, our manager added us on a school tour. While on tour we dropped our first single called "Gualla" which landed us a digital distribution single deal with eOne Music formerly Koch Records. Unfortunately, Hurricane Boyz didn't work out so we decided to go our separate ways.

**Q. Wow, so did you ever work or meet with Souija Boy after the group you was in won the contest?**

A. No, it was a contest on his website. He put our faces and music on the front of the website which was receiving millions of hits at the time.

**Q. Dealing with your experience with Koch Records, do you feel like an artist can succeed without a record label and all you need is good management?**

A. Yes, because today's era is based off of social media compared to a few years ago when you needed labels to put your music in stores. Now it's easier to reach out to the consumers.

**Q. How did you become apart of the Street Hitta DJ Movement with Big Dawg Blast and what do you have in store for us this year?**

A. I got a good support system from family, from past relationships with Big Dawg Blast from FM98 WJLB. He hosted our last mixtape which was the perfect combination and he recently heard some of my new material. I'm completing my album Mac Sauce, touring, and performing.

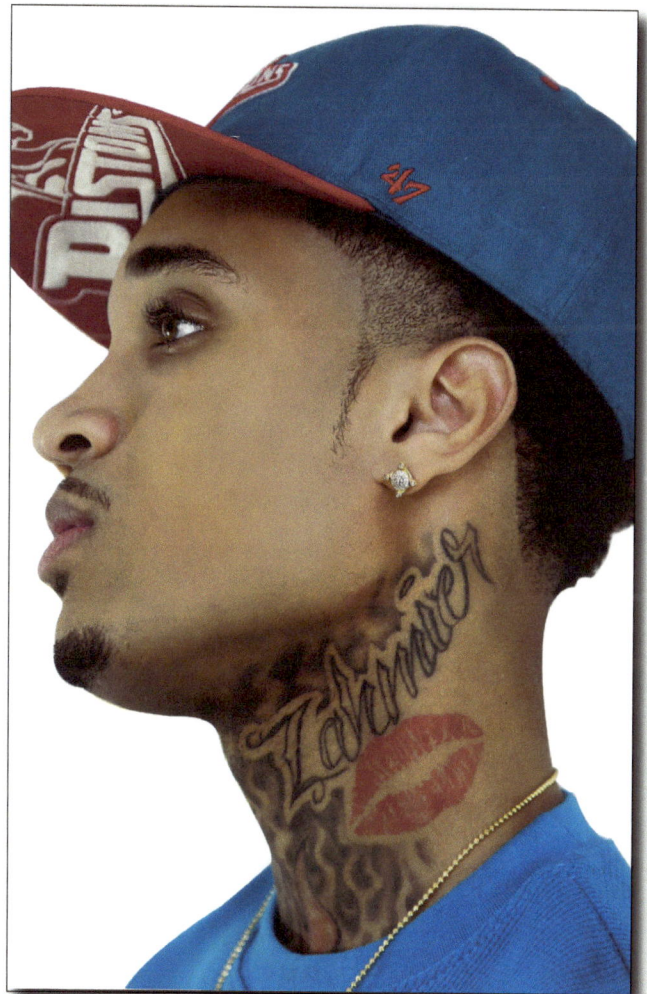

# D-Town Triple Treat Gucci Rie

## THE MULTI- TALENTED RAPPER, ACTRESS, AND MODEL TALKS ABOUT HER 24/7 GRIND AND HER UPCOMING ROLES IN THREE INDUSTRIES.

**by Cheraee C.**

**Q. Who is Gucci Rie as an artist and how do you plan to impact the music industry?**

A. I am the rap diva bringing change to the game. the beauty, the bold, the message... I want all to relate to me so I use my creativity as top tool. It's been a journey finding my place in this game, but I found it and the time is now. The stage is mine! I plan on being one of the greatest entertainers of all time! I most definitely do this for the women of the world! We hold so much power! Time to sit the bad b*tchhh down and rise the queens. New music coming soon; the life behind my smile. My heart is forever on the line now. You will hear her roar! #IAMGUCCIRIE

**Q. Besides music, what are some of your other crafts and how do you manage to balance time for crafts other then music?**

A. I just stepped into the acting scene...Yes I love it! My birth name is Riel! so it's her time to shine finally. I was always confused on who Riel really was... I found her and fell in love! New D-TOWN actress (yeaaa now I get to use all my krazy personalities lol) #swing hair. Thanks to the Remarkable Mark Hunter and Stacey J for giving me the start of my best experience in productions. I did my first stage play with them and it's a honor to work with amazing writers and directors. Let It Burn and Consequences, I got to play the over the top Neka; the Hilarious girl who got them bundles on deck and Lisa the crazy babymama. What an experience! I'm hooked now!!! You looking at top lady actress yo with the leading lady attitude #swing hair. Movies, here I come, claiming the victory in advance. I can do all things!!! You can do all things just believe it and do it!!! There you have it triple threat diva!!! Actress/Rapper/Model... How do you manage them all? They are my life, my reason, my purpose. I'm built for this task... I'm goin make it look easy #crownme!

**Q.. How did you come this far and what exactly do you do day to day to make all things possible?**

A. Sacrifice!!! Coming into the game I didn't know that it was a full-time job. I wasn't ready, but I wanted this I was passionate, determined, and dedicated, I gave it all I got. No breaks; I sacrifice sleep, friends, and my time. I was married to the game!!! I did not have all the answers, but I know I wanted people to know my name so I started branding myself and took every stage possible. I put out 4 mixtapes and quit my job to put in the 24/7 grind. Sometimes it's a struggle, but I keep the faith so I can't lose. I rather put all my energy to my dreams and goals then working for somebody who probably don't appreciate you anyway. It's amazing to know you got fans and people who you inspired (love it)! I block the haters and focus on the love: my motivation. If you love Gucci Rie I promise I won't disappoint you. I'm on a mission going straight to the top #comewithme!

# Old Skool Entertainment Inc.

RJ SCOTT IS FAR FROM YOUR AVERAGE EVENT PROMOTER
3-IN-1 PACKAGES TAKING OVER THE MIDWEST AND MORE.
by Cheraee C.

**Q. A lot of people promote events so what makes you standout from other promoters?**

A. I provide a service unlike other promoters that's what I call "A Night Out on the Town." I purchase pre-sale tix to the hottest events locally and international; secure transportation-including limo service depending on the size of the group, and arrange dinner. I call it a 3-in-1 entertainment package! My packages could include event tix, dinner, and limo. This past NYE, I did party bus, hotel, and Hollywood Casino Concert.

**Q. What is the biggest event you've ever promoted in terms of turnout and celebrity status?**

A. I just promoted/hosted a 3-day, 3 venue "Blues Tribute Weekend" in the D honoring Detroit's own blues legend John Lee Hooker. Again again, please refer to my website, click on the event title top of my homepage for more events. I promoted Keyshia Cole (here in Detroit.) A package that included limo pick up/ overnight hotel stay, and concert at Motor City Casino/Hotel at the Soundboard after concert and meet and greet with photos with Mrs. Keyshia Cole just to name a few!!!

Please visit my website for an overall pic of what we do @ www.oldskoolentertainmentinc. com.

Old Skool Entertainment, Inc. Will Promote/Host
**A BLUES TRIBUTE WEEKEND IN THE D WITH DETROIT'S OWN LEGEND JOHN LEE HOOKER**
THE TRUE KING OF BLUES

# The Midwest Diva Takes The Stage

MOBDIVA THE FIRST LADY OF STAY READY ENT HAS HER EAR TO THE STREETS AND STAY READY TO TAKEOVER THE STAGE

by Cheraee C.

Q. How long have you been chasing your dreams in this fierce music industry?
A. I've been rapping since I was 8 years old. I didn't get serious until 2004 when I dropped my first album "Street Diva."

Q. Who was your plug? How did you get as far as you've gotten in the industry?
A. Lol, I'm my plug! My hardwork and drive to succeed! I've always paid for my own studio time and basically anything associated with my career. My 1st major feature I gladly paid for was with Detroit legend E-Dub and then Dogmatic. They helped to get me noticed and respected as a serious artist when I first started my career. Since then my husband and business partner S. IXX holds my career on his back! Together we have created a plug for our community and it feels great to give back while pushing myself further as well.

Q. Since you have a partner with your husband, how do you balance your career and your relationship and what is a typical day in your world like?
A. Kinda like that Rihanna song Work, Work, Work, Work! It's kinda crazy trying to balance it all, but we figure it out! We really need our old reality show Out Tha Box TV back on the air! I'm kinda passionate about my music to put it lightly.

Q. Being on TV is a big thing, what happened with the reality show and what channel did you air on?
A. Out Tha Box TV was a local cable show, but reached thousands of viewers through Ch. 19 CTN Ann Arbor. It aired two years straight from 2008-2010. It was a Hip Hop reality style show with local rap showcases! The success of the show led to the birth of our video production and photography services and the show had to take a back seat to the coins, but were back with Ear2dastreets.com another platform for local artists to showcase their talents including yours truly!

Q. Will the show be returning or do you have some other ventures planned just as great?
A. Maybe! I'm hoping to do many things this year along with releasing a single I'm working on with the

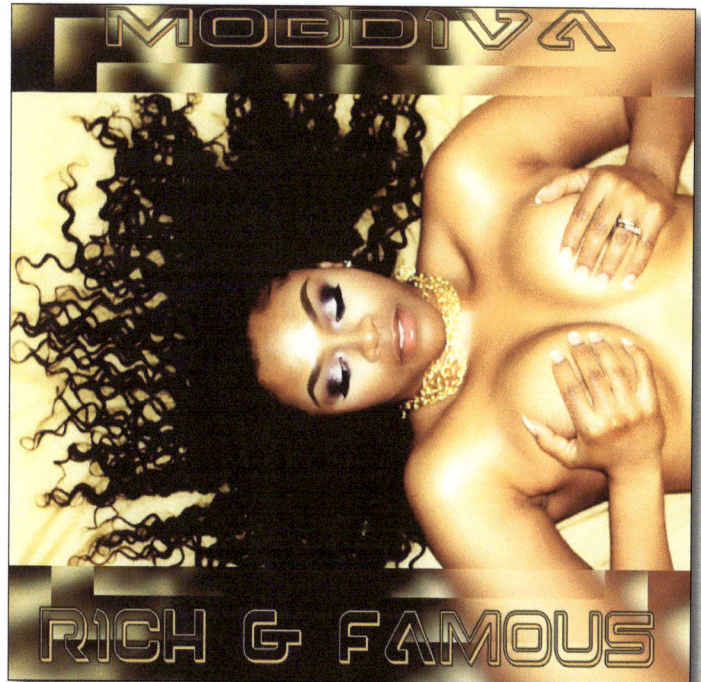

Olympicks! I've been doing a lot more local performances lately as well and now giving my own shows with some really cool promoters. My next show is April 24th at Crossroads with DJBJ Mr.3525; Ear2dastreets.com will link with Victory Entertainment for the 2nd time. Then we're super excited to bring out La'Britney to EMU for The Queen of Diamonds Showcase brought to you by fearless Soul Entertainment and Ear2dastreets.com. I can't wait to showcase my new msuic and along with some club favorites like "Rich & Famous" produced by Ken Flav. I will also be in Jackson, MI at the Jackson Theatre with Iam_Merlo so things are steady and I'm just waiting on my 8 mile moment! LOl.!

*Photography by Keith O Brien*

# The Sony/ATV Share

SONY BUYS OUT MICHAEL JACKSON'S ATV MUSIC PUBLISHING SHARE.

by **Semaja Turner**

The legendary Michael Jackson who has been resting in heaven since 2009, use to own a 50% share of Sony/ATV. In 1985 Jackson brought ATV Music Publishing for a whopping $41.5 million dollars, and in 1991 Jackson sold 50% of his stake in ATV to Sony for $100 million dollars to form Sony/ATV which was the smartest investment in music history. Since then EMI Music Publishing has been added to the music publishing empire. Now Sony has purchased Jackson's share for around $750 million dollars. Sony is the largest music publising company in the world and owns the rights to many greats and legends such as The Beatles, Beyonce, Lady Gaga, Taylor Swift, and many more.

Not only was Michael Jackson the King of Pop, but he was the king of investing in music publishing the way he doubled his dividends and some. It's not like Sony/ATV is the only music publishing company that MJ invested in anyways. MJ's portion of his share will help pay off the debt he had acquired before he died and the rest of the money will be put into a trust fund for his three children.

# JP ONE Tha Chosen One

## THE GIFTED AND TALENTED LLC CEO IS MAKING MAJOR MOVES ALL OVER THE MIDWEST WITH THAT REAL MOTOWN MUSIC.

**by Cheraee C.**

**Q. What's been going on with you since your last interview in the 2nd issue of SDM?**

A. I released Fire and Brimstone 3 to more rave reviews, and even better sells than expected. I went on a couple successful promotional tours. Then, me and Nep Jennings started working on a joint effort, Real Motown Music. We ended up with more great music than we expected, so we released the EP, first to our mailing lists and then to the general public. The response was incredible. We just released the video for "Bass" and the Real Motown Music Album will be dropping soon.

**Q. You were honored at this year's Underground Hip Hop Awards. Describe that experience and what awards you received?**

A. Yes, I received the MVP award from The Underground Hip Hop Awards. It was a great experience. Last year, I was nominated for three or four awards and I didn't make the Top 5 in any category. This year, I made the Top 5 in a few of the categories I was nominated in, including Best Lyricist and Best Full-Length Album (for Fire and Brimstone 2.) Progress is a process. I'm not focused on winning awards as much as I'm focused on building my fan-base, but everything counts. #westillwinning

**Q. Word on the street is its some issues with you and Big Gov so what's the truth behind that?**

A. To be honest, I ain't meet Gov until 2012, but I knew a lot of his family from Southwest, though. I recorded a verse for Nubian Mady, a Reggae artist from Sengal, when I first came home. Jeanna Tall, who hooked it up, told me that he liked the verse, but the studio quality wasn't that good, so Nubian Mady was going to come to Detroit and record the song over. She was working with Gov, so they said we could record it at his studio. Gov jumped on the song too. After the song was complete, him and Nizguy refused to turn the masters over to Nubian Mady and his management. Me and Gov were still cool, but some FB stats and sneak disses happened and we had a small fallout in 2013. He swore he wasn't

shooting at me, so I let it be. We kicked it and did the song, "Fuck Your Feelings" for his album that was supposed to come out a couple months later. He said I could use it for my Gifted and Talented album too, which was supposed to come out later in the year. His album never came out, so the song ended up looking like my song. I got a little steam with "Nuttin' Like Me" (ft Jeter aka Bruce Wayne) and I wanted to follow it up with the Gov feature. He said he'd get the video shot, so we started shooting the video and never finished. He blamed it on the director, but I found out that he told the director that he wanted to do something else. He had me fuck up my roll out for nothing. I would've gotten the video shot. I shot a few promo videos and then shot the "Fuck Your Feelings" video, anyway. A few more incidents occurred that ensured me that Gov was never going to let me get ahead, so I asked a few people who've dealt with him a lot longer than I have and they let me know I wasn't crazy. Some of his family from the hood had already warned me, but I had to see for myself. I just created a lot of distance and once someone asked him why I wasn't fucking with him, he asked me what was wrong, and I let him know that we're different. I want everyone around me to win and he's all about Gov. I turned off my Facebook page for two months and when I turned it back on, I seen Gov doing Gov: sneak-dissing, making it like I used him to get my own momentum and then said fuck him. We threw a few shots online, but when I seen him, he was all peace. A day later, he was back at it, so I aired him out. Ain't no beef; he's just different. I'm really from Southwest. No one fucks with him in the hood. I know real BMF niggas and none of them co-signs his BMF lie. I never seen him mention being a Crip until he started rocking with Trick-Trick.

Q. So do you think y'all will reconcile and do more music or you just goin keep moving up in your lane?
A. Gov is one of the most talented people in the world, but I've learned that succeeding in this business ain't about talent. If a nigga can call me "brother" and "family" and impede my progress, I can't trust him, so I'll never work with Gov again. We've made some dope music, but that's it. I wish him and his team the best, though.

Q. How did you get the name JP ONE and what does it represent?
A. JP One is a Y2K version of Jackpot Tha Chosen One. Most people from the streets and prison still call me "Jackpot." I started using that as a stage name in 2000. I was in negotiations with Barrett Strong, who is a Hall of Fame writer/singer for Motown and I was calling myself ACH Tha Jackpot. I did about a year in juvie and when I came back, he said, "before you left, you were just Alvin, now you're Jackpot!" I thought about it and dropped the ACH and just used Jackpot. I was working on my debut album "Tha Chosen One," so I would say that on the songs I was recording. The album was never released, but after a while, I just adopted the moniker into my stage name. While I was locked up, I started writing my logo on my rhymes, instead of signing them. It's a JP1 in the logo and once I learned about marketing, I realized it was easier to use JP ONE, instead of Jackpot Tha Chosen One. Still means the same thing, just easier to manage.

Q. Are you single, married, or just focused on chasing your dreams?
A. My relationship status is very complicated. Let's just leave it at that. It's not something I'm proud of and it's not something I'm ashamed of either. I just try and keep it out of the public. I had two kids by two different women last year, and I make sure the kids and their mothers are great.

Q. What other projects can we expect from you besides Real Motown Music?
A. I'm working on a script for a short-film and a book. The Fire & Brimstone Trilogy will be released as a box set with all three albums, a few bonus cuts, and a DVD with all of the visuals from the projects. I'm not looking to release any more albums this year, but I'm always recording. I'm looking forward to a lot of quality features and exploring more of the business side.

Q. Thanks for keeping it real with SDM, can you give us one reason why you rocks with SDM?
A. I rock with SDM because they have always rocked with me. I have every other issue and I'll have a few of this one hanging up somewhere. This is my first cover and I know it won't be my last. I appreciate all the love.

# TOP 10 CHARTS

## TOP 10 DIGITAL SINGLES AND ALBUMS
### APRIL 1, 2016

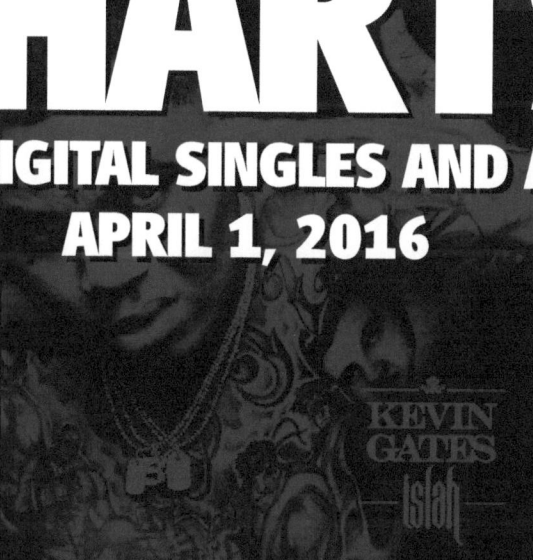

# TOP 10 CHARTS

DESIIGNER IS ONE OF THE YOUNGEST RAPSTARS OUT TODAY WITH HIS NEW SINGLE "PANDA" .

## TOP 10 SINGLES
## CHART OF THE MONTH

| No. | Artist - Song Title |
|---|---|
| 1 | DESIIGNER - PANDA |
| 2 | YO GOTTI - DOWN IN THE DM FT. NICKI MINAJ |
| 3 | JEREMIH - OUI |
| 4 | J COLE - NO ROLE MODELZ |
| 5 | KANYE WEST - REAL FRIENDS |
| 6 | NEISHA NESHAE - ON A CLOUD |
| 7 | YUNG THUG - BEST FRIEND |
| 8 | DRAKE - SUMMER SIXTEEN |
| 9 | MOBDIVA - RICH AND FAMOUS |
| 10 | CHRIS BROWN - LIQUOR |

## TOP 10 ALBUMS
## CHART OF THE MONTH

| No. | Artist - Album Title |
|---|---|
| 1 | KEVIN GATES - ISLAH |
| 2 | TWEET - CHARLENE |
| 3 | DAVID BANNER - BEFORE THE BOX |
| 4 | BRYSON TILLER - TRAPSOUL |
| 5 | FUTURE - EVOL |
| 6 | KANYE WEST - THE LIFE OF PABLO |
| 7 | TYRESE - BLACK ROSE |
| 8 | TANK - SEX, LOVE & PAIN II |
| 9 | J. COLE - 2014 FOREST HILLS DRIVE |
| 10 | AYE MONEY - SDM COMPILATION (VOLUME 2) |

# ALBUM REVIEW

KEVIN GATES
islah

## Islah

**ARTIST:** Kevin Gates
**REVIEWER:** Cheraee C.
**RATING:** 4

The Louisiana rapper Kevin Gates is back with more of his lovey, thuggish, conflicted, but realistic bars. He named his latest album Islah after his eldest daughter Islah which is an Arabic name that means to improve, to better, or to put somethhing into a better position.

His tracklist includes the radio banger 2 Phones, and bangers including Really, Really, Time for That, Thought I Heard, The Truth, Excuse Me, and Jam featuring Trey Songs, Jamie Foxx, and Ty Dolla Sign. I give his album five stars.

**RATE METER:  1 - WACK  2 - NEEDS WORK  3 - STRAIGHT  4 - BANGER  5 - CLASSIC**

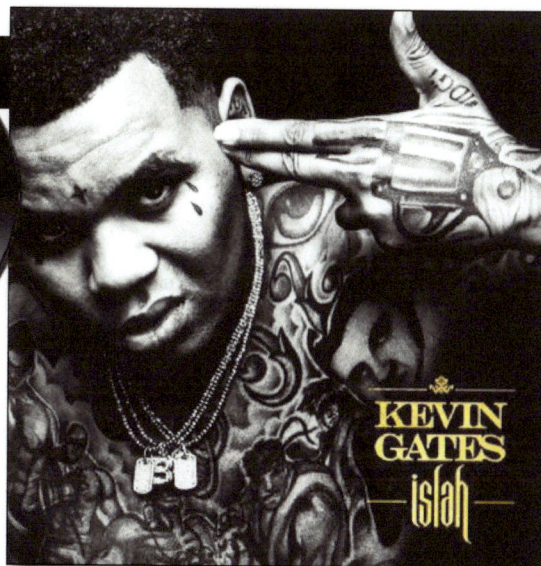

tweet
CHARLENE

## Charlene

**ARTIST:** Tweet
**REVIEWER:** Cheraee C.
**RATING:** 3

Tweet took a break from the industry for over 10 years and now she's back with her 3rd album and has reunited with Missy Elliott and Timbaland. Her tracklist includes tracks from Somebody Else Will featuring Missy Elliott, Magic, Won't Hurt Me, Priceless, The Hardest Thing, and more. I give her album four stars.

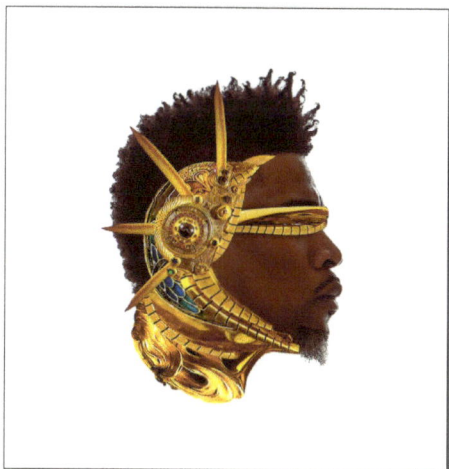

## Before The Box

**ARTIST:** David Banner
**REVIEWER:** Cheraee C.
**RATING:** 4

David Banner seems to have taken a new direction in his lyrics aimed toward politics and global issues in everyday society. Tracks include Marry Me, Evil, In the Wind, Malcolm X, Amazing, Swag, Cross, Warrior, BTL, My Uzi, Pain, and more. I give his album four stars.

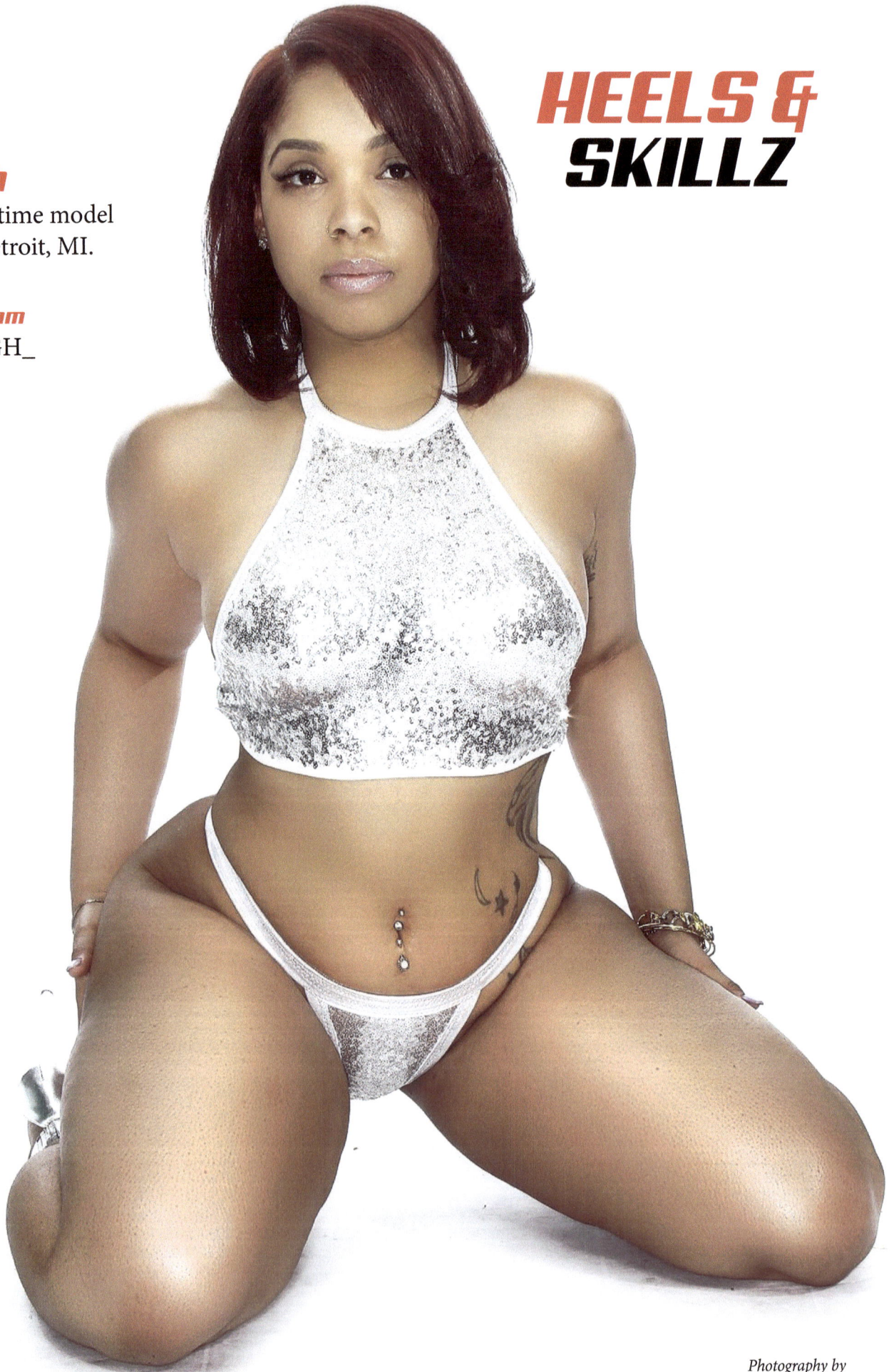

**HEELS & SKILLZ**

**Leigh**
is a full-time model from Detroit, MI.

*instagram*
@_LEIGH_

*Photography by*
@barearmy

# HEELS & SKILLZ

**Cierra**

is a beautiful model from Detroit, MI.

*instagram*
@_cierra

*Photography by*
@barearmy

# HEELS &
## SKILLZ

**Da Truth**
is a sexy model
for barearmy and
lives in Detroit, MI.

*instagram*
@DATRUTH101

*Photography by*
**@barearmy**

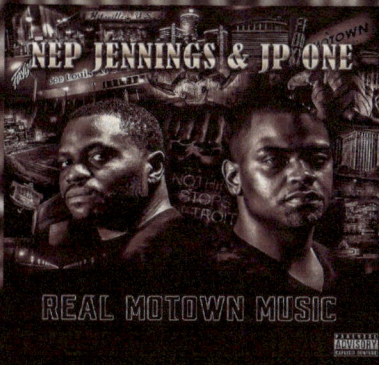
# MotorCity Radio

**SDM SAT DOWN WITH TERRY MARTIN TO CHAT ABOUT LEGACY WITH R&B AND HIS NEW RADIO SHOW AND SHOWCASES.**

**by Semaja Turner**

**Q. So Terry, how did you get into doing radio and showcases?**
A. I started out as a manager of an artist: Kendrick Hardaway, an R&B vocalist and there was not many., if any opportunities for singers to perform in Detroit. At that time Detroit was a mostly rap town. The only shows were rap showcases and talent shows so we created our own show. One that caters to R&B artists, wasn't an open mic or karoke so the whole goal was to make and sustain opportunities for artists in Detroit who did R&B.

**Q. Have any of the artists that have been in your showcases or your radio show made it?**
A. Regionally, there are several who sing background for Charlie Wilson, Kem, Tyrese, and opened up for Lalah Hathaway poetry. A few have moved to LA and ATL where they have continued working as writers or producers. Charity Ward was signed by Dime's label. Kai Fears is a backing dancer for Charlie Wilson.

**Q. What is going to be the next showcase you have and who's going to be in it?**
A. The next show is April 22, 2016 featuring Johnyce Jackson, Aaron Williams, Mason, and from Richmond, VA T-Soul.

**Q. When your not on the radio or doing your showcases how do you spend your time?**
A. Father, husband, plant life... I work for the Big 3... I'm a marcking band head. I got my start in music at Mackenzie High School marching band then Southern University. I've always been a music head. Love discovering new artists. It's always been about creating opportunities for artists especially Detroit artists to blossom. R&B Live Detroit Soul and the City Radio Show, the Blog, RnB in the D... It's all Detroit love.

# NEXT 2 BLOW

## *HICKSGATE*

**Q.** Your artist name Hicksgate is very interesting. What is the philosophy of your name?
A. My last name is Hicks and there's a big roundabout near Bristol called "Hicksgate Roundabout." I failed my first driving test there so people started calling me that haha.

Q. How do you feel about Hip Hop in your country? Is Hip Hop overrated or underrated?
A. The last few years we've started to have more British artists making music which can compete with American shit so we're finally getting some recognition. It's all about the quality of music. Right now we need more UK artists setting the bar as high as they can so we don't fall back into irrelevance. That's why I'm here lol.

Q. Who would you compare your sound too in Hip Hop today and what is your view of Hip Hop today?
A. People who inspire me at the moment are Travis Scott, Skepta, Kendrick, and Thug. I try to compare myself to artists at the top because I'm trying to reach that level. But my view of Hip Hop has always been as a fan from halfway around the world so I'm just vibing that so much dope music is being released.

Q. As an international artists is there any limitis to the places you will venture to in your career?
A. Nah man I wanna go anywhere that lets me through the border.

Q. What steps have you taken to be a national recording artist?
A. I'm just trying to push as much as possible now. Been focused on improving my music for 3 years and now its at a good level. I'm ready to get it out there and start gigging wherever wants to turn-up.

Q. What can we expect from Hicksgate in this prosperous year of 2016?
A. Some next shit! I want people to get excited when  they hear my name so we're just gonna carry on dropping bangers until everybody knows.

**Q.** How long have you been pursuing your rap career and where are you from?

A. I popped up in the underground scene in 2013, and that's when I started to take it serious. By people's choice I didn't realize how much of an impression I was gonna leave every time I stepped off a stage. I was raised in Roseville, MI.

Q. It's not many white females artists in the industry so what are you bringing to the table?

A. As soon as I have a mic in my hand I think the race thing gets thrown out the window. I think what it is with white rappers: whether it be male or female is how authentic can she be because I'm doing something that is mostly an African-American and male dominated sport if you will because it is definitely a sport., but for me its a Hip Hop cultural thing and I just happen to be Caucausion, not a black and white thing.

Q. It seems like you are very comfortable in your skin, and your position in the industry. so tell us what reflects your music?

A. I wasn't put together by well-oiled machine of an industry that taught me how to do this or speak like that. I'm just me and confident about who I am, I was told by a fan that I'm something different for girls to look up to. You don't need a 20 inch waist and a fake butt to create a fanbase. I rep for every girl that was what she told me. "She can't accomplish her dream because she is a particular size, sex, or color." I'm big, beautiful, and confident. I feel sexy and my music usually reflects that, no aplogies. At the end of the day its about that raw talent and work ethic, and in this case you get both.

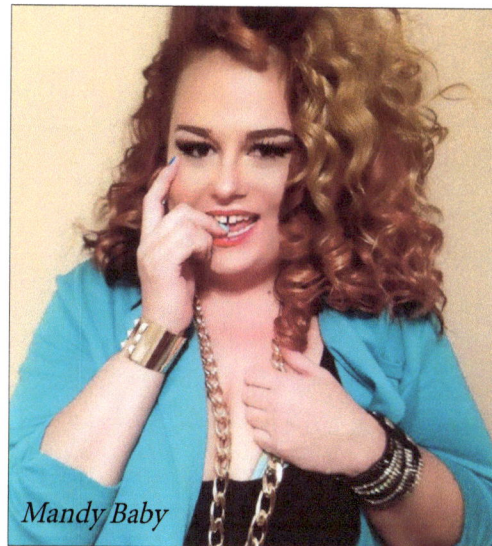

*Mandy Baby*

Q. Why don't you drop a couple of bars and pretend like you on the mic.

A. Yea it's camera time, but it's not your time. Call me a thief I'ma take what's mine. No time for lames and they all the same. Thinkin they gon change the game? So they mad at me cus I'm different? Be mad at me cus I'm winning! But man fuck they feelings cus Mandy Baby bout to get eeemmm!

*Woodrow*

**Q.** Who is Woodrow and define yourself as an artist?

A. Woodrow is a mutli-talented Artist/Producer/Recording Engineer/Actor from the westside of Detroit. As an artist I would define myself as a well-rounded/versatile legend in the making! (Yea I said it.) I make my own beats, I write my own music, and other ppls music as well. I engineer, mix, and master all my own music as well as others. Woodrow's music has an "industry sound" that meshes between east coast lyrics with a southern twist. Thats who Woodrow is.

Q. Who is Woodrow outside of music and all the other crafts and hats that you wear?

A. I was a student athlete in high school. I played for Ferndale Alt High School who went 23-2 and won 2nd place in the 2008 state tournament. I am a proud father of 3, 2 girls and one boy. I am really interested in branching off into acting as well.

Q. You say you are a versatile legend so what makes you so versatile and a legend?

A. I can do more than just one style of music. I have a range of hip hop records, hip hop/r&b/pop sounding Top 40 type records. I make my own beats, I self-promote, and throw my own events. That's what makes me versatile. I feel like I will be a legend in my own right. Not too many people have the capabilities that I have and I won't settle for anything less than greatness. When its all said and done I will be a legend. You gotta move with that kinda confidence you know?

# SNAP SHOTS

**Email Your Snap Shots to**
snapshots@sdmlive.com

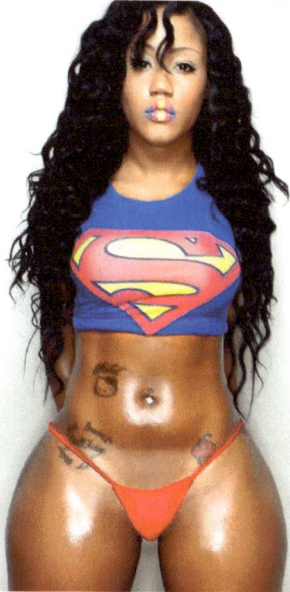

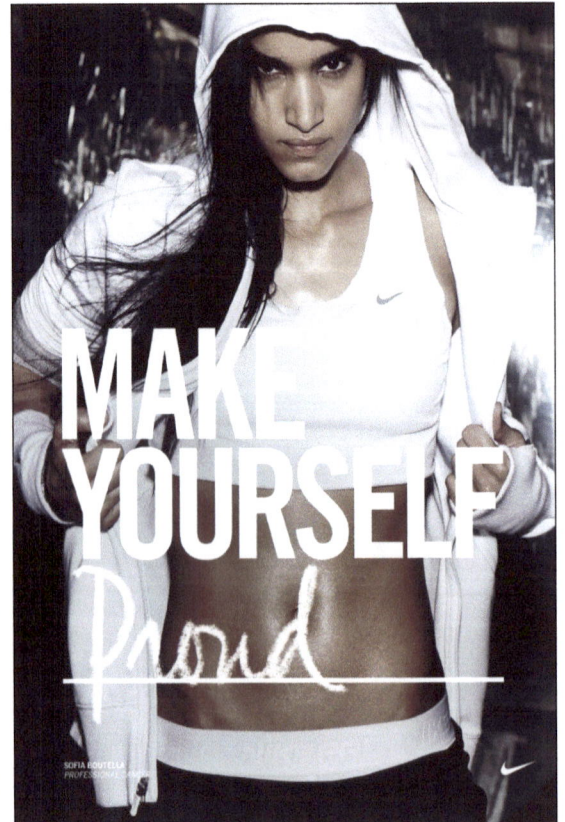

MAKE YOURSELF Proud

SOFIA BOUTELLA

# WE HAVE THE LOWEST PRINTING PRICES IN THE NATION

## 250 EVENT TICKETS
FULL-COLOR ON BOTH SIDES ON THICK UV COATED 14 PT

only $45

## 1000 BUSINESS CARDS
FULL-COLOR ON BOTH SIDES ON THICK UV COATED 14 PT

only $25

## 1000 4X6 CLUB FLYERS
FULL-COLOR ON BOTH SIDES ON THICK UV COATED 14 PT

only $65

Need a Design? Add $20 for Business Card or $40 for Flyer

## 2x5ft VINYL BANNER
FULL-COLOR IN or OUTDOOR BANNER w/GROMMETS

only $99

## 5000 BUSINESS CARDS
FULL-COLOR ON BOTH SIDES ON THICK UV COATED 14 PT

only $99

## 2500 4X6 CLUB FLYERS
FULL-COLOR ON BOTH SIDES ON THICK UV COATED 14 PT

only $85

CHECK OUT MORE SPECIALS & ORDER ONLINE ANYTIME: WWW.5DSPRODUCTIONS.COM

1.888.718.2999  5DS PRODUCTIONS®
THE PRINT MEDIA CENTER.

*THE ALL NEW STYLE OF MAGAZINE-BOOKS*

**SDM**

www.ingramcontent.com/pod-product-compliance
Lightning Source LLC
Chambersburg PA
CBHW040020050426
42452CB00002B/56